KINGDOM INSIGHTS
for Fathers

5 Strategies for Building a Lasting
Relationship with Your Children That
Fosters Love, Respect and Honor.

JESSE A. COLE, JR.

Copyright © 2025 by Jesse A. Cole, Jr.

All rights reserved. No part of this publication may be reproduced, distributed, or transmitted in any form or by any means, including photocopying, recording, or other electronic or mechanical methods, without the prior written permission of the publisher, except in the case of brief quotations embodied in critical reviews and certain other noncommercial uses permitted by copyright law.

All Scriptures are taken from the New International Version (NIV) translation unless otherwise stated.

ISBN 13: 978-0-9847798-8-8

Printed in the United States of America

Book cover design by Jesse A. Cole, Jr.

Contact Info:
Jesse A. Cole, Jr.
info@CoachJesseCole.com
www.CoachJesseCole.com

Dedication

To My Father
Your presence in my life has been one of the greatest advantages I have. Though you did not have a father present in your life, you made a decision to break that cycle, and for that, I am forever grateful. Your commitment to being available, your sacrifices, and your example have shaped the man I am today.

To My Coaches and Mentors
To the men who poured into me—coaches, teachers, pastors, community leaders, and friends—you each played a significant role in my journey. Your words and actions have left an imprint on my life, and for that, I honor you. May this book be an extension of the lessons you have taught me and be passed down to future generations.

To Young Men and Future Fathers
My prayer is that this book equips you with wisdom, encouragement, and a renewed sense of responsibility to embrace your role as a father and leader in your family and community. You are needed. You are valuable. You are called to lead with purpose and confidence.

With gratitude and purpose,
Jesse A. Cole, Jr.

Contents

Introduction 8

A Father's Presence Establishes Identity 12

A Father's Presence Releases Confirmation 19

A Father's Presence Develops Legacy 31

A Father's Presence Establishes Emotional Value 40

A Father's Presence Brings Security 48

Conclusion 58

Additional Resources 60

About the Author 65

KINGDOM INSIGHTS
for Fathers

5 Strategies for Building a Lasting
Relationship with Your Children That
Fosters Love, Respect and Honor.

JESSE A. COLE, JR.

Introduction

Being a father has been one of the hardest, most rewarding assignments I've ever had. I know that you might be saying, "What a way to start a book," but if you know, you know.

Although I've had a combination of healthy and unhealthy male examples and have received plenty of advice on fatherhood, there was no textbook or workshop that could've prepared me for the joys and challenges of being a father. It's just something one has to experience for themselves to truly understand. Being a father has taught me more about myself than anything else. It has been an exercise of spiritual, emotional, and personal development.

One thing I do know is that our children need us. As much as society tries to downplay the power of a father's presence and as the government is sanctioning the reconstruction of what a father is, our children need to see us in action to understand the rhythm of a man, how we move through life, and the way we handle tough times. They need to hear our voices because a father's words and tone help to shape how a child receives instruction. They need the ambiance of our energy because it brings with it a sense of security. They need to feel our touch to understand the purity and perfect balance of strength and gentleness. There are just certain aspects of a man that can't be manufactured or redefined. The essence of manhood can't be explained. It can only be experienced and then passed on by a man.

I don't claim to be an expert on fatherhood nor is this book an attempt to build a platform. I'm simply being obedient to what God told me to do: encourage men to be visible and involved in the lives of their children. If this book had a foundational statement, the heart of this message would be for men to see and embrace their value as fathers. Whether you live in the home with your children or in a different location, they need to know that you want to be in their life. Your presence impacts every aspect of their being.

The National Center for Education found that students perform at a higher academic level when a father is actively engaged in their lives. This is true for biological fathers, stepfathers, and single-parent fathers. The Fatherhood Project, a non-profit program that empowers fathers to be knowledgeable, active, and emotionally engaged with their children, researched specific impacts of father engagement during childhood development stages. One thing they found is that the quality of the father-child relationship matters more than the specific number of hours spent together. Another data point revealed that high levels of father involvement are correlated with higher levels of sociability, confidence, and self-control in children.

There are also spiritual examples of fatherhood that we must consider. Many of the Biblical leaders we read about were present fathers. Although flawed, they understood their responsibility to lean into God for direction as they led their children. Noah was a father who stayed close to God in practice and in deed (Genesis 6:9–10). When given the vision to build the ark, he led his wife, their three sons, and their wives on a mission to change the trajectory of the world.

Job, known for his faith and perseverance through affliction, was a father who honored God with his time and provided a lifestyle for his children that was rewarding (Job 1:1–6). And even though he lost his first set of children, God saw fit to give him more. However, the best example of a father is God. Through His example, we witness the power of presence and the blueprint for love—a love that is sometimes expressed through affirmation, and other times through accountability. Either way, His love remains pure, unconditional, and everlasting.

Deuteronomy 6:6–9 provides a picture of the sense of awareness a loving father has when leading his children in the way of the Lord:

> *"These commandments that I give you today are to be on your hearts. Impress them on your children. Talk about them when you sit at home and when you walk along the road, when you lie down and when you get up. Tie them as symbols on your hands and bind them on your foreheads. Write them on the doorframes of your houses and on your gates."*

We have to be vigilant about not passing down toxic philosophies that were taught to us or indoctrinating our children with the unhealthy beliefs we learned through trauma. Both will cause our bloodline to remain stuck in a way of thinking that perpetuates generational deprivation. However, in the Scripture above, Moses is projecting a sense of urgency as it pertains to teaching children the ways of God. We'll talk more in depth about this later.

One of the most important things we can do as a father is provide sound instruction. Our children depend on us to contribute to the narrative for their lives and to help shape their world. We must never stop communicating with them and giving them the opportunity to hear our heart and the space to share their ideas.

Many great men have contributed to my success. Whether family members, coaches, teachers, church leaders, or community leaders, each played a unique and significant role in my growth and development as a man. However, my first example of manhood was my biological father. As a kid, I was lucky enough to have him present in my life. Many of my friends didn't have the same privilege, and I recognize that I was fortunate. He didn't grow up with a present father in his life, and one of the promises he made to himself was that he would be present for his children. At the time of this writing, he is still an active source of wisdom I can plug into.

Throughout my life there have been experiences I've had with my father and other men that had a profound impact on me. The lessons I gained from these experiences, in combination with God's Word, drive me today as I am leading my wife and children and coaching leaders in my business. Some of these encounters serve as the backdrop to the insights I share in this book.

Whether you're currently a father to your own children, dream of being a father, or you're a father figure, you are needed and necessary. My prayer is that you are inspired to incorporate these principles into your life in a way that honors God, builds your confidence, and helps your children thrive.

Salute!

Chapter 1

A Father's Presence Establishes Identity

"My father didn't tell me how to live; he lived, and let me watch him do it."

- *Clarence Budington Kelland*

My earliest memories of my father are him being gone for work, studying for sermons, cooking barbeque ribs, fishing, and attending my little league basketball and football games. He didn't have a present father figure in his life, so for him to be intentional about being available for his wife and children was a conscious decision he made. Him being there gave me a sense of identity. When I was younger, we didn't talk much about what being a man means, but I watched him demonstrate manhood in front of me.

He wasn't and isn't a perfect man—none of us are—but through him, I got the chance to see what it looked like to dream, work through family challenges, start businesses, manage a household, pastor churches, work in your passion, and be involved in the community.

I would watch him study his Bible for hours. That taught me the importance of knowing the Word of God. He showed me what it looked like to work diligently toward a goal, and how to adapt and be resourceful.

He was and is a respected leader in our church community, and because of his reputation, I was exposed to a wealth of opportunities that helped me grow my confidence to use my gifts on big platforms. On occasion, those experiences called for me to do hard things, but he was right there, not saying many words but encouraging me with his presence.

These lessons are the foundation for how I lead my family today. My passion for sharing my insights and experiences with leaders is a result of watching him spend hours constructing a sermon and then standing in the pulpit to preach it. A big part of who I am is because I watched him.

A father plays a key role in helping his children find their identity and empowering them to meet expectations. I don't have a lot of memories of my father verbally speaking into my life. However, his actions showed that he was proud of me as a son, and I never felt like I was a disappointment.

As I'm now raising children of my own, I can see the value of actively and verbally pouring into my children, intentionally reinforcing who they are, and holding them to a high standard. I believe children need to know the intrinsic value they possess because the world is efficient at telling them that they aren't good enough. But when a father buys into the importance of identifying and articulating their child's worth, it erects a pillar of confidence that the child can always lean on. The truth is, children find themselves in their father. What an awesome connection!

In Matthew 3:16–17, we see God openly affirming Jesus. In the middle of a baptism ceremony, God spoke into his identity, confirming a major step in His ministry. Here's the scriptures account of what happened:

> *"As soon as Jesus was baptized, he went up out of the water. At that moment heaven was opened, and he saw the Spirit of God descending like a dove and alighting on him. And a voice from heaven said, "This is my Son, whom I love; with him I am well pleased."*

Although they are separate in function, there is no separation between Jesus and the Father (John 5:29). Jesus is the expressed image of God. When you see Him, you see the Father (John 14:7–11). They are one in the same. Jesus embodies all that is God (Colossians 2:9). As a person who has put their faith in Jesus, we have been given the same access as Jesus to the Father.

> *We are made in His image (Genesis 1:27).*
> *We are accepted (Romans 15:7).*
> *We are complete (Colossians 2:9–10).*
> *We are one with Him (1 Corinthians 6:17).*
> *We have work to do (Ephesians 2:10).*

Because of our relationship with the heavenly Father, we can offer the same access to our children. Their identity is a reflection of their relationship with us. When we embrace the magnitude of this reality, it empowers us to live in a way that pleases God and supports our children, helping them to experience God through us and providing a healthy example for how they can parent their children.

When my son, Dean, was a baby, I'd recite an affirmation over him during bath time. After cleaning him, I would lift him out of his baby bathtub, wrap him in a towel, and speak the following words over him:

I am a King. I add value to the world. I have self-control, self-respect, and integrity. I am the master of the choices that I make. I will not blame others for my mistakes. I am responsible for my future, and I embrace my destiny. I am a King. I am smart. I am a leader. I help people, and I love Jesus.

As he grew, he eventually began saying them with me. Just as God declared Jesus' identity, I did the same for my son. I recited that same affirmation over my daughter, Nya, when she was a baby—only I replaced "King" with "Queen."

My brother, your presence is essential to the survival of your child. There is no substitute for it. According to a study done by the National Fatherhood Initiative, "Children with involved fathers have a strong foundation for child well-being. They are at lower risk for teen pregnancy, emotional and behavioral problems, neglect and abuse, obesity, low school performance, incarceration as juveniles...," and a host of other issues. Of course, there is an adverse effect when the father is absent.

There's something about getting a nod of approval from a father that gives a child the courage to take on the world. Your children are a reflection of you, but more importantly, they are a gift from the Father. They don't belong to you, so you must steward them properly.

Chapter Discussion Questions

1. Do you consider yourself a present father? Why/why not?

2. When was the last time you verbally communicated how proud you are of your child? What was their response?

3. Do you think your presence matters to your child? Why/why not?

Chapter 2

A Father's Presence Releases Confirmation

"As fathers, we know that our children need our love and need our guidance and need our faith in them. We know that our children need from us what only we as fathers can provide them."

- Hendrith Vanlon Smith Jr.

Merriam-Webster defines *confirmation* as "the process of supporting a statement by evidence." This implies that a person or entity must have prior knowledge of—or have witnessed—an act or event, thereby gaining the authority to vouch for its validity. As fathers, we hold the power to acknowledge the gifts, talents, and calling of our children, exercising the authority God has entrusted to us to affirm and endorse them. Let's revisit Jesus' baptism to reinforce the focus of this chapter.

In Matthew 3, we find John the Baptist in the wilderness preaching and teaching about the importance of water baptism and repentance. His ministry was in part to prepare the way for Jesus' leadership, which involved baptizing with the Holy Spirit. In verses 13–15, Jesus walks onto the scene to be baptized by John. With respectful resistance, John pushes back on Jesus' request because he didn't feel qualified to perform such a task. However, Jesus reminded him that it must be done to "fulfill all righteousness." It was only after Jesus said this that John consented to baptize Jesus.

The Greek translation for "righteousness" is *dikaiosynē,* which means "the approval of God" or "divine approval," the state of being in proper relationship with the Father. Verses 16–17 provide us with a glorious picture that encapsulates this act of obedience from Jesus and the heart of the Father.

> *"As soon as Jesus was baptized, he went up out of the water. At that moment heaven was opened, and he saw the Spirit of God descending like a dove and alighting on him. And a voice from heaven said, "This is my Son, whom I love; with him I am well pleased."*

This moment marked the start of Jesus' public ministry. You would think that it got better from this point, but as soon as He was baptized, the Holy Spirit led Him into solitude where Satan was waiting for Him.

Matthew 4:1 tells us that Jesus was led into the wilderness to be tempted by the devil. After fasting for forty days and forty nights, He was hungry. In Matthew 4:1–11, we witness the enemy attempting to exploit a perceived weakness to derail Jesus from His assignment. Yet, every time the enemy presented an unrighteous alternative, Jesus responded with a righteous response. Verses 3 through 11 highlight the epic exchange between Satan and Jesus, ultimately revealing the evidence of God's confidence in His Son.

³ The tempter came to him and said, "If you are the Son of God, tell these stones to become bread."

⁴ Jesus answered, "It is written: 'Man shall not live on bread alone, but on every word that comes from the mouth of God.'"

⁵ Then the devil took him to the holy city and had him stand on the highest point of the temple.

⁶ "If you are the Son of God," he said, "throw yourself down. For it is written:
"'He will command his angels concerning you,
*   and they will lift you up in their hands,*
*   so that you will not strike your foot against a stone.'"*

⁷ Jesus answered him, "It is also written: 'Do not put the Lord your God to the test.'"

⁸ Again, the devil took him to a very high mountain and showed him all the kingdoms of the world and their splendor.

⁹ "All this I will give you," he said, "if you will bow down and worship me."

¹⁰ Jesus said to him, "Away from me, Satan! For it is written: 'Worship the Lord your God, and serve him only.'"

¹¹ Then the devil left him, and angels came and attended him.

This exchange shows us the human side of Jesus. After being tested, He had the strength to go public with His ministry. How does all of this relate to the heart of this chapter? Just as God confirmed Jesus' identity when He said, "This is my Son...," we have the power to do the same for our children.

If I were to borrow from the account of Matthew 3:17, it would sound like this, "These are my children, Dean and Nya. Everything that I am, they have access to. They walk in my authority, and I authenticate and affirm their purpose. I am well pleased with them."

When we affirm our children, it gives them all of the rights and responsibilities that come with being connected to us, their father. One of the highest forms of leadership we can have is to confirm our children's identity in Christ. When we do this, it guides how we parent them because we know that our children don't belong to us. We're just stewarding their lives. It gives them permission to show up in all spaces knowing who they are, and they'll be less likely to submit to being tagged with an identity that only serves other people's agenda.

In John 14, Jesus was having a critical conversation with His disciples about His soon departure and return. He made a statement that illuminated His identity to them. In verses 3–4, he said, "And if I go and prepare a place for you, I will come back and take you to be with me that you also may be where I am. You know the way to the place where I am going."

Stunned by this, Thomas said, "Lord, we don't know where you are going, so how can we know the way?" (v. 5). Jesus responded, "I am the way and the truth and the life. No one comes to the Father except through me. If you really know me, you will know my Father as well.

From now on, you do know him and have seen him." (vv. 6–7).

How was Jesus so certain about His assignment? I believe God's endorsement empowered Him to operate in the fullness of Himself. Likewise, when we confirm our child's identity, it gives them the confidence to release the spirit of authenticity onto their friends and acquaintances, which is a freedom that only comes from the Father, released to you, their father. Because God confirms our identity, we can confirm theirs.

Children also look to their fathers to confirm their dreams and ideas. There is no limit to their imagination and aspirations. Your presence can make them feel like they can do anything and everything at the same time. Let's be honest, if you grew up with a loving father or positive male figure, you may have felt the same way, but then life got a little more complicated. You tasted the bitterness of "reality." There are dreams you once had, and because life happened, those dreams have either died or are lying dormant. This can cause resentment, and if you're not careful, you can unknowingly project those bad feelings and emotions onto your children.

I don't believe that any loving father would purposely do this, but bitterness has the tendency to seep out in ways you never imagined. Resentment impacts our sleep, keeping us in a perpetual state of exhaustion, and exhaustion affects our mood, which influences how we communicate with our children. When a man doesn't feel valuable, it's hard for him to see value in others, including his children. It's dangerous for us to view our children through exhausted eyes because the faults we see in ourselves can become magnified in them. Maybe this isn't your story, but I can relate.

Probably one of the most challenging times for me as a father was when Dean was six years old. I was struggling to connect with him, and I couldn't understand why. My mind was consumed with shame, and I was having a trouble sleeping. Then, one night around midnight, I felt a prompting from the Holy Spirit to go grocery shopping. So, I got out of bed, got dressed, and told my wife I was heading to the 24-hour Walmart a few miles away from our house.

As I was walking down the freezer aisle, the Holy Spirit hit me with a haymaker: "Jesse, you're parenting your son from a place of fear, not love. That's why you can't connect with him." As soon as I heard this, I stopped in the middle of the aisle, slouched over my grocery basket and started crying. Every effort I made to connect with my son was failing. Whether it was teaching him how to ride his bike, dribble a basketball, or read a sentence, I was in a constant state of frustration because it seemed like he wasn't learning the lessons fast enough. What the Holy Spirit showed me was that my childhood was totally different than his.

Growing up in the inner city in the late '80s and early '90s, there were certain unspoken rules that existed that kept you alive. I'd been in many fights and other compromising positions because the environment that I lived in was more about survival than safety. This produced a sense of paranoid awareness that I still carry to this day. When it came to parenting my son, I attempted to teach him certain lessons not for the sake of learning a life skill but so that he wouldn't be seen as weak and naïve. I didn't want him to become an easy target.

As I stood in the middle of Walmart, slumped over my grocery basket, God checked my heart, and I embraced the freedom to parent my son out of love, not fear. He showed me that Dean will not have the same experiences I had as a child, so there was no reason to be afraid for him. I could teach him the same lessons and skills, but the motive of my heart must be pure. It had to come from a posture of love, not fear. Because I was projecting my anxiety onto him, he couldn't receive my instruction in love, and that was the disconnect.

Children look to their fathers to confirm that they are loved. Love has to be present in order for it to be distributed. One may ask, "How do I give pure love when I've never received it?" That's a great question. If you're a man who has never experienced the pure, masculine love of a father, it may be hard to identify it within yourself and even more of a challenge to give it to your children. So, you're left with the task of trying to find the love that you missed as a child.

That's how gang culture thrives. It feeds off of the lack of identity and the need for young men and women to feel loved and accepted. Because of this deficiency, the gang is able to create a sense of community with rules and regulations that perpetuate its mission.

So, for the man who is struggling to understand how to love his children, I'd point him to the Father. Through embracing and submitting to His love, we learn what real love is versus a manufactured love that has been redefined to fit our expectations or someone else's agenda. He is the source of all things good. He is the power that wipes away the infirmities of our past so that we can have hope in who we're called to be. He is a loving, patient Father, and we can be the same.

Love is a learned behavior and a conscious choice we make, and 1 John 4:7–12 is a prime example of this:

> *"Dear friends, let us love one another, for love comes from God. Everyone who loves has been born of God and knows God. Whoever does not love does not know God, because God is love. This is how God showed his love among us: He sent his one and only Son into the world that we might live through him. This is love: not that we loved God, but that he loved us and sent his Son as an atoning sacrifice for our sins. Dear friends, since God so loved us, we also ought to love one another. No one has ever seen God; but if we love one another, God lives in us and his love is made complete in us."*

In John 15:9, we see Jesus expressing the power of God's love for him, which empowered Him to love us in the same way: "As the Father has loved me, so have I loved you. Now remain in my love." A father's love for his children sets the tone for how they love themselves and others. Love does not start with a feeling, although we can express love through emotion. Love is more than an action, although we can manifest our love through various demonstrations. Love is a decision we make. It means that we've identified true love as being a reflection of God's character.

Regardless of the circumstances, we can adopt His example of love, being thankful for the benefits and being willing to grow through the challenges that love sometimes presents. What does this mean for us as fathers? It means that we love our children whether they make wise choices or not. We may not always agree with their decisions, but we can agree to love them and show it through our words and actions. Constructive encouragement is just as important as constructive criticism. Yes, there may be consequences for their behavior that does not align with the standard, but our children should always know that they are loved, and the consequences must be rooted in love, not fear. The world does a great job of condemning them. Knowing this, we have an opportunity to counter that condemnation with graceful correction rooted in our devotion to the Father.

In 1 Corinthians 13:4–8, Paul defines how we can demonstrate love in a practical way:

> *"Love is patient, love is kind. It does not envy, it does not boast, it is not proud. It does not dishonor others, it is not self-seeking, it is not easily angered, it keeps no record of wrongs. Love does not delight in evil but rejoices with the truth. It always protects, always trusts, always hopes, always perseveres. Love never fails."*

What an awesome opportunity we have as fathers to practice speaking into our child's identity, confirming their dreams and ideas, and securing their confidence in us to love them like God does. I'm hopeful that as you're reading this, God is speaking to your heart, and I gracefully challenge you to be obedient to what you're hearing and have a sense of urgency toward applying His instructions today! I pray that He gives you the best words to say to deepen your impact as a father.

Chapter Discussion Questions

1. In what ways are you helping your child live in their God-ordained identity?

2. What are your child's dreams and how are you actively supporting them?

3. After reading this chapter, what is God specifically saying to you about confirming your child?

Chapter 3

A Father's Presence Develops Legacy

"The greatest legacy one can pass on to one's children and grandchildren is not money or other material things accumulated in one's life, but rather a legacy of character and faith."

- Billy Graham

As a former educator, I've served in multiple roles. From substitute teacher, Dean of Students, in-school suspension coordinator, parent liaison, basketball coach, and college student success coach/mentor. I've had hundreds of conversations with students about their habits, behavior, their hopes and dreams, and the importance of remaining focused on their academic responsibilities.

Many of these conversations centered around the presence of a father in their lives or the lack thereof. In almost all of the interactions, regardless if the student was male or female, they cited how important their father was to their development, even if they held contempt for him. They intuitively understood how critical their father's presence—or his absence—was to their success and survival.

One of the most impactful encounters I had was with a student. To protect his identity, I'll call him, Ron. Ron was the first in his family to go to college, and he came to my office for guidance around navigating the challenges that many freshmen experience.

He had spent the last five years bouncing between the streets and high school, but he was getting exhausted with that life. However, even though he was frustrated, he wasn't totally committed to being a full-time college student either.

During our coaching session, he shared that his father had died several years prior to him graduating high school. Before his passing, he and his father were going through a rough patch, but he tried his best to be present. Ron's face lit up when he talked about him. I sensed that he had a deep affection for him, and I could tell that this young man loved his father, even though he didn't have the ideal relationship with him.

As he continued to share his story, the Holy Spirit gave me words of comfort and accountability to give to him. Here we are sitting in my office on a college campus, and a routine coaching session turns into a spiritual intervention. I can't remember the exact words I said to him, but whatever they were, they made him reflect, and then he started to cry. He said, "What you just said to me sounded like something my dad would say to me." It was as if God used me to get a message to him in his father's voice. We got up from my desk, I asked to give him a hug, he consented, and he sobbed a little more. I felt like God was working through me to give him the touch of a father. As he walked out of the room, I made a note to follow up with him. Although I sent several emails and left a few voicemails, he never scheduled another session, but I'm confident that he got what he needed that day. Sometimes our job is to be the bridge to someone else's breakthrough. A source of encouragement and confirmation.

Why did I share this story, and what does it have to do with legacy? Unfortunately, my student's father didn't get the opportunity to live long enough to see him graduate from high school, but the little time he spent with his son left a mark on his life. If you're reading this book and your child is still alive, you have an opportunity to be physically present for them. Whether you live with them or not, or you've made mistakes that cause you to feel unworthy to be a father, your presence is a legacy pillar. I like how Tim Ross, the creator of The Basement Podcast, said it: "The right man doesn't need that much time to leave an indelible mark."

This is what I call a Kingdom-centric legacy. It is an intentional effort to be authentic about pouring your life into the life of your child. It is a form of succession. It's when a father makes the decision to give his child as much wisdom as they have the capacity to retain because he understands that they'll need it one day. Even if they don't see the value in it now, the seed you've planted will be profitable for them in the future.

A Kingdom-centric legacy does the following for our children:

1. **A Kingdom-centric legacy gives our children a starting point.** We must be intentional about creating a clear pathway for them to have a chance to win. They will indeed have their own challenges, but they shouldn't have to carry ours and theirs at the same time. Your legacy is a piece of their inheritance (Proverbs 13:22).

2. **A Kingdom-centric legacy intentionally sets the moral compass for our children.** Allowing God's Word to influence our parenting gives our children insight into God's character, which shapes how they respond to the world (Ephesians 6:4).
3. **A Kingdom-centric legacy points our children to God as the source of all things**, not their job or even another person (1 Corinthians 8:5-6).
4. **A Kingdom-centric legacy purposely prepares our children to effectively lead others.** As we teach them about God's heart and character, they will spread this knowledge to their friend groups, directly and indirectly impacting those around them through word and deed (1 Timothy 4:12).
5. **A Kingdom-centric legacy teaches our children how to honor us as parents.** As we teach them how to honor God, consequently, we teach them to honor us. As they mature, they will begin to see the correlation between their heavenly Father and us, their earthly father. This may not always be a perfect relationship, but when we properly and intentionally establish the foundation, it gives them a chance to grow into understanding the place of honor (Proverbs 22:6).

Legacy indicates that there was a concerted effort to develop a structure to serve as the foundation for a desired future. Those who were committed to laying the foundation faced immense challenges, but their hope for the future caused them to sacrifice their blood, sweat, and tears so those coming after them wouldn't have to endure those same hardships.

A closer observation will show that there is a dual responsibility at play here. The recipients of legacy have a responsibility to learn about those who paved the way, and the ones who've selflessly formed the core structure have a responsibility to document the process and pass along the principles they've learned so that the next generation can run with the baton, building upon their work.

Your presence as a father gives your children a point of reference for what a godly legacy could be. Their relationship with the heavenly Father is directly connected to how they engage with you. The example you set is the window to their future. They will learn how to frame the world through your eyes first.

When asked if there was any data showing the effects of successful black fathers who were actively present for their children, Roland Warren, president and CEO of Care Net and the former president of National Fatherhood Initiative replied, *"I don't know of any specific statistics that have tracked that…my view is kids have a hole in their souls the shape of their dads."* I see the value in that sentiment.

A 2022 study done by The Center for Disease Control (CDC) notes that the average lifespan of men in America is 74.8 years old. When you do a basic internet search, you find that on average, a man becomes a father at the age of 30. These numbers fluctuate based on race. As a black man, my life expectancy is 63 years old. At the time of this writing, I am 46 years old. My children are ages 10 and 8 years old. According to these numbers, I only have about 17 years left with my children.

Let's be clear, I pray for a long life, and I've made adjustments in my diet and exercise routine that can have a positive impact on my overall health. My plan is to kiss the faces of my grandchildren and shower them with love. But I have to be real with you—when I saw that I have less than twenty years left to be with my children, that number made my heart drop, and I started to think about ways to redeem the time I've wasted with them and how I can be intentional about being present in the future even in the seemingly smallest ways.

I encourage you to do the calculations for yourself and make the necessary adjustments to make every day count. There is a piece of legacy on the inside of you that your children need, and it can only be passed on to them when they are in close proximity to you. Many adult children are struggling because their father never passed the baton. Don't wait for them to ask you for the wisdom. Create opportunities to pass it along to them, even if you feel like they may not understand it yet.

The Holy Spirit has the power to bring it back to them at the right time. Your responsibility is to plant the seed. Additionally, make a conscious effort to document your thoughts, philosophies, and beliefs so that when you die, they don't just have memories of you, but they have your words in your voice. If you're reading this book, you still have time. Act with purpose and create the framework that will feed generations to come. Licensed Professional Counselor Craig D. Lounsbrough said, "A father is the man who can change a world he will not be part of by building the tiny human that is part of him."

The fragrance of your legacy prepares the way for your children, giving them the spiritual and practical tools to be healthy adults. It establishes God as their source and which gives them the confidence to lead others by living an authentic life. When they honor God, they honor you in the process. And that's something you can be proud about.

Chapter Discussion Questions

1. In your own words, why is it important to leave a legacy?

2. How are you intentionally sharing your experiences and ideas with your child?

3. How can you better maximize and enjoy time with your child?

Chapter 4

A Father's Presence Establishes Emotional Value

"One of the greatest lessons I learned from my dad was to make sure your children know that you love them."

- Al Roker

    The family dynamic typically finds the father being the disciplinarian. Let's be honest, we spend a lot of time instructing, correcting, or troubleshooting. Throw in a few raised voices, spankings, and stern looks, and you've painted an accurate picture of how we've traditionally been represented as fathers. Simply put, most of our daily interactions with our children aren't graceful experiences for them or us.
    Truth be told, fatherhood can be exhausting at times. Because we are both naturally and supernaturally wired to establish and maintain order, it can feel like we're constantly managing, repairing, or preparing—just to keep things from falling apart. Couple that with us being so used to working with our hands and living in our head that it becomes difficult to tap into the heart of what being a father truly means from an emotional aspect, which is the part that helps us connect with our children on a deeper level.

Children rely on fathers to deposit into them emotionally, but it can be difficult to offer them our affection when our own emotional bank hasn't been filled. Men are often trained to conceal their feelings, as revealing them is seen as a sign of weakness. For generations, we've been taught this unhealthy method of coping, only to pass on characteristics that contribute to the breakdown in communication with our families.

When we fail to do the work of connecting with our emotions, we won't have the capacity to help our children identify, articulate, and manage theirs. Being brave enough to acknowledge our relational growth gaps and areas of opportunity helps us to guide our children down the same pathway.

Alex Karras, former NFL player and TV dad on the sitcom, *Webster*, said, "It takes more courage to reveal insecurities than to hide them, more strength to relate to people than to dominate them, more 'manhood' to abide by thought-out principles rather than blind reflex. Toughness is in the soul and spirit, not in muscles and an immature mind." Here are some ways fathers can strengthen our emotional intelligence, which in turn help our children do the same.

Acknowledge What You're Feeling

Being able to identify what you're feeling gives you a starting point for articulating and managing that feeling. If you've determined that you're angry but you don't want to be, you can regulate the emotion by identifying why you're angry and then incorporate solutions like breathing exercises, positive affirmations, and Scripture that address the root of your anger.

In Proverbs 16:32, Solomon writes, "Better a patient person than a warrior, one with self-control than one who takes a city."

If counseling is needed, don't be afraid to pursue that option too. Whether anger, rejection, abandonment, joy, fear, love, or sadness, acknowledging your feelings gives you the tools to help your children identify and work through their emotions effectively.

Be Open to Feedback

We all have our own ideas and ways of doing things. But sometimes we can have blind spots that are preventing us from maximizing our potential. God loves you so much that he's assigned people to your life who have the capacity to support your growth, and their feedback could be of value to you. But if you get offended or you're too proud to receive it, you could miss a quantum leap in your growth as a man and as a father.

James 1:19–20 provides insight into how to receive feedback: "My dear brothers and sisters, take note of this: Everyone should be quick to listen, slow to speak and slow to become angry, because human anger does not produce the righteousness that God desires." Listening to learn versus listening to defend yourself will help you develop a skill that can grow your influence with your child.

Communicate with Grace

As present fathers, there are two key variables we must consider that determine successful outcomes when communicating with our children: our expectations and our tone. We have to remember that our children have not lived our lives. They are learning how to live their own. They don't see the world the way we see it, so we can't be married to our expectations of them. When we have unrealistic expectations for our children, we can get frustrated when they don't meet them. That emotion can impact the tone in which we communicate.

Our tone has just as much impact as our words. Communicating with our children through the lens of frustration can cause more damage than good. Projecting our anger onto them forces them to bear a weight they don't have the capacity to carry.

Frustration implies anger, irritation, bitterness, and disappointment, which are derivatives of the fruit of the flesh. But the fruit of the Spirit is love, joy, peace, longsuffering, kindness, goodness, faithfulness, gentleness and self-control (Galatians 5:22–23), and they all align with God's grace. When we communicate through the fruit of the Spirit, we are planting seeds in the hearts and minds of our children.

In Colossians 4:6, Paul writes, "Let your conversation be always full of grace, seasoned with salt, so that you may know how to answer everyone." Stay positive. Hold the standard, focus on the process, not perfection. Speak to their future, not their past. This type of communication is Spirit-led. A father's emotional deposits into his children will soon manifest through their actions.

Research suggests that when children learn to steward their emotions around the age of four, they become emotionally aware adults. In an article published by Psychology Today entitled, "Father Absence, Father Deficit, Father Hunger: The vital importance of paternal presence in children's lives,"[1] it states, *"...children consistently report feeling abandoned when their fathers are not involved in their lives, struggling with their emotions and episodic bouts of self-loathing."*

Emotional empowerment from a father builds confidence in the child. When we do our own emotional development work, we are empowered to model the practices and results for our children.

---

[1] https://www.psychologytoday.com/us/blog/co-parenting-after-divorce/201205/father-absence-father-deficit-father-hunger

Chapter Discussion Questions

1. How do you usually cope with emotional exhaustion?

2. Who are the people in your life who have permission to hold you accountable?

3. Have you ever responded to your child in a harsh tone? How did they respond? How did you feel about it?

Chapter 5

A Father's Presence Brings Security

"The nature of impending fatherhood is that you are doing something that you're unqualified to do, and then you become qualified while doing it."

– *John Green*

In the previous chapter, I talked about how part of our responsibility as fathers is to create an environment where our children feel safe enough to talk to us. Their quality of life is contingent upon them being raised in a home where they are secure, seen, and at peace. As a father, you have the power to create this type of environment.

When children aren't raised in a safe, peaceful, and stable home, they are more likely to indulge in destructive behavior including drug and alcohol abuse, risky sexual practices, domestic violence, and unproductive social habits. This is not always the case, as there are some children who will defy the odds, succeeding regardless of their conditions. These are the outliers. There have also been children who were well taken care of but have made destructive life decisions.

So, to assume that a safe home will dictate whether

or not a child will live a long, productive life would be unfair. But I stand by the idea that children have a much better chance at making healthy life decisions when they are raised in an environment where they feel safe, secure, and seen.

In 2003, I was hired as the K-5 Dean of Students at Pontiac Academy for Excellence in Pontiac, Michigan. I was a little over a year removed from graduating college. I had worked a few part-time temporary jobs, even did some substitute teaching for a while, but this was my first real job. I remember getting my first check. It was around $900, and I thought they made a mistake because I had never earned that much in two weeks. I went to my human resources representative to make sure the amount wasn't a mistake. She chuckled and said it was right. In hindsight, I should've known how much I was supposed to make, but I was a twenty-two-year-old trying to figure life out.

In a lot of ways, this position was my introduction to fatherhood. As the Dean of Students, my responsibilities included managing the lunchroom, which meant I was charged with developing a system that ensured that each lunch period ran smoothly. On any given day, I was either cleaning tables, sweeping floors, mopping up vomit, creating games to play to keep the students occupied until their teachers came to pick them up, or teaching a life lesson.

The other part of my job required me to create and implement a student code of conduct, which meant that I had to manage and enforce the consequences of disruptive behavior. Depending on the level of disruption, a student would either spend the remaining portion of their class period in my office finishing their work, their parents would be notified of their behavior, or they would get suspended from school for a specific amount of time. When I was in the middle of doing this work, it was frustrating. But looking back on my experience, I grew as a man and leader.

One morning, a third grader walked into my office. He had dried up tears on his face and a referral slip in his hand. A referral is a behavioral report given by the teacher to a student who has been disruptive in the classroom. This document provides a detailed account of the incident, outlining what happened and the steps the teacher took to try to address the behavior.

The young man who walked into my office was not new to this process. In the past, he had been sent to me for yelling at another student, inciting a fight, and sleeping during instruction time. Although this wasn't my first encounter with him, it would turn out to be the most memorable. Little did I know that day would change our relationship, as I would come to learn more about his challenges at home that contributed to his behavior.

When I read his referral, it mentioned that he had been sleeping in class. So I asked him about it, and the conversation went something like this:

> Me: *Your referral said you were sleeping in class. Is this true?*
>
> Student: *Yeah.*
>
> Me: *Why were you sleeping in class?*
>
> Student: *[Lip smack] Because I'm tired, and I'm hungry.*

Me: *I understand. But school just started. Why are you tired and hungry?*

Student: *Because I didn't sleep good last night, and I didn't eat nothing for breakfast.*

Me: *Ok, why didn't you sleep good, and why didn't you eat breakfast?*

Student: *Because my momma and her friends be loud all night. They be listening to music and smoking all night, and me and my sister can't get no sleep. They be eating all the food too.*

As we were having this conversation, his head was on the table, and his eyes were closed. I gave him a snack and let him sleep in my office until he felt better. When he woke up, we had lunch together, and I learned more about him and his background. He shared that missing meals and sleepless nights were common for him and his sister. His father wasn't present, and he didn't have a positive male figure in his life.

I attempted to reach his mother via phone several times that day but was unsuccessful. Later, I spoke with his teacher and the school's social worker to give them some insight into why he was continuously disruptive, and we talked about ways we could partner to help him stay engaged in class.

Some days I'd give him an extra sandwich or fruit at lunch, other days I'd ask the cafeteria ladies to set aside snacks for him to take home in his backpack for him and his sister. There was even an occasion when he came to school with his pants falling down because he didn't have a belt, so the social worker went to the store on her lunch break to buy him one. We wanted him to know that he was cared for, even if he didn't make the best grades. The most important thing we could do for him was to preserve his dignity and provide a safe space for him to grow and learn.

I could share plenty of similar stories of students who came from challenging backgrounds who were negatively impacted by their conditions, but this one sticks out to me because it was one of my first encounters that taught me about the effects of adults mishandling their responsibility to foster a healthy environment for children. In 2019, the Substance Abuse and Mental Health Services Administration (SAMHSA), through the National Child Traumatic Stress Initiative, released a report providing research-based information on the prevalence and impact of traumatic events on children. The report found that the effects of trauma include the following:

- Learning problems, including lower grades and more suspensions and expulsions.
- Increased use of health and mental health services.
- Increased involvement with the child welfare and juvenile justice systems.
- Long-term health problems (e.g., diabetes and heart disease).

Both parents play a significant role in changing the narrative of this data, but fathers have been empowered with the mandate to lead the charge towards establishing secure boundaries. We must take ownership of it.

In Luke 15, Jesus shared a parable of the lost son. This young man lived in comfortable conditions but longed for a different life detached from the rule of his father and the watchful eye of his older brother. A life where he would be in control of his destiny. When reading this story, we are often focused on his selfish desire to exercise his independence, and it's easy to skip over the provision of his father. Although this story isn't based on real people, the principles that Jesus teaches are fruitful.

Verse 12 gives us insight into the character of the father. The son says, "Father, give me my share of the estate." This implies that the father had done the necessary work to create a life for his children that was secure and free of unnecessary stress. The son had everything he needed to thrive under his father's care.

After the father gave him his portion of the estate, the son went out and wasted it all on wild living. When the money ran out, so did his friends. He found out that the world didn't love him as much as his father did, so he swallowed his pride and started his journey back home. Verses 20–24 capture the heart of the father and the purpose of this chapter.

> Verse 20: *The father sees the son coming home and runs to him to embrace him.*
> Verse 22: *The father covers and restores the son.*
> Verse 23: *The father makes provision to feed the son.*
> Verse 24: *The father makes peace with the son, creating a safe space for him to come back home to.*

I believe this is an accurate picture of God's design for fatherhood. To create a space where our children feel safe enough to make mistakes and seen enough to know they matter. Accountability pierces through the armor of rejection, and it can be received when the leader has intentionally placed grace at the point of the spear.

Grace is God's way of reassuring us of His love, even when discipline is present. Likewise, your presence is the security that locks out the elements that threaten the livelihood of your children, and it protects and preserves the culture that supports it.

I decided to do a search on my former student to see if I could find him. It's been over twenty years since our encounter, but I can still see his tear-stained face. It took me a few days of sifting through social media profiles and doing multiple Google searches, but I found him. My heart dropped when I saw his name listed on the Michigan Department of Corrections website. He had been charged with Domestic Violence and Assault with a Dangerous Weapon. At the time of this writing, he is twenty-eight years old. Fortunately, he was released from prison in 2023.

One can't help but wonder: what if this young man had a responsible adult male at home when he was a child? A man who understood the impact his presence would have on the children in that house and the family at large. What if he knew what it felt like to be raised in a safe environment where he was protected, fed, and seen?

I'm praying that one day I'll get to see him again. I'm not sure if he'll remember me, but I'd love the opportunity to tell him how his life has impacted mine. And if he has a family, I would be honored to encourage him to be the father that he didn't have.

Chapter Discussion Questions

1. Do you feel qualified to be a father? Why/why not?

2. What are some of the practices you've established to ensure your child is safe, seen, and protected?

3. Do you feel like you've created a safe space for your child to fail? Why/why not?

Conclusion

I'm thankful that you've finished this book. It means a lot to me that you would dedicate time away from your work and family to flip through these pages. I hope you got what you needed.

If I can be real with you, this was probably the hardest book I've written to date. One reason is because prior to being led to write it, I was just living it. When you're in the thick of the process, you're learning as you go. I'd never documented my thoughts or even considered my guiding principles as a father. There are no key performance indicators to measure my success against a set of predetermined goals or what other fathers are doing. Of course, my foundation is God's Word, but I've also tried my best to incorporate the good things I've learned from my father and other men in my life while also noting their mistakes and not repeating them.

Like most men who are trying their best, I've had to reprogram my thoughts and reevaluate my expectations. As Father God is deepening my understanding around fatherhood, I'm learning that this journey isn't about making it comfortable for your children. Sometimes you have to tell them *"no"* so that you can train them to steward your *"yes."* Sometimes you have to be the lion (set order, be firm, give tough love) so they can appreciate the lamb (grace, patience, long-suffering, etc.)

As Hebrews 12:11 teaches, "No discipline seems pleasant at the time, but painful. Later on, however, it produces a harvest of righteousness and peace for those who have been trained by it." Through it all, as fathers, our motive is to always parent from a place of love. I've experienced a few MVP moments, but for the most part,

I'm just trying to make sure I stay in the game. Keeping a consistent regiment of reading and applying God's Word, listening to worship music, fasting, investing in books, watching Kingdom-inspired content, and fellowshipping with other fathers has kept me sharp. Without these tools and outlets, I'd be as dull as a butter knife trying to cut through a steak.

    I hope this book serves as a companion resource as you walk with God to solidify your presence in your child's life. Whether you're a new father or an experienced one, you have been called to a specific assignment. Your presence serves as a marker for your child to revisit and a point of reference for them to build on.

    You are qualified because He called you to it. You are a son of the King. There is no lack in the Kingdom of God. Everything you need to be a great father has already been established. May these insights serve as a reminder of God's love and His intentional plan to make you one with Him so that you can hear His heart for your child and execute your assignment from a posture of grace.

Additional Resources

Questions That Every Father Must Answer

God wants you to have His heart for your child. Sit with Him and ask the questions listed below. Listen to the answers He gives you, write them down, and be obedient to doing the next step.

1. Father God, am I parenting out of love or out of fear? What do I need to do to lead my child like you'd have me to?

   _____
   _____
   _____
   _____
   _____
   _____
   _____
   _____

2. Father God, how can I establish a legacy of love with my child?

   _____
   _____
   _____
   _____
   _____
   _____
   _____
   _____

3. Father God, what does it look like for me to be intentional about getting to know my child for who you created them to be.

_____
_____
_____
_____
_____
_____
_____
_____

4. Father God, in what ways can I extend grace to my child?

_____
_____
_____
_____
_____
_____
_____
_____

Discussion Questions for Father's and Their Children

These questions are meant to open up dialogue between you and your child. Listen to their words but hear their heart. This is not a time for you to get defensive or your chance to correct them but an opportunity to listen and guide them with grace. You are listening for how they think, not what they think. If you don't agree with their answers, refrain from downplaying their perspective, over-talking them, or dismissing how they communicate their thoughts. Do your best to validate even the smallest piece of truth they share, and trust that God will create an opportunity for you to course correct when necessary. On the lines below, write down what resonates with you the most about their answers.

1. In what ways can I be a better father for you?

_____
_____
_____
_____
_____

2. What are your goals and dreams, and how can I support you in accomplishing them?

_____
_____
_____
_____
_____

3. What do you value more: gifts from me or spending time with me? Why?

_____
_____
_____
_____
_____
_____

4. What would you like to know about my life as a kid?

_____
_____
_____
_____
_____

5. What don't you like about me? Why?

_____
_____
_____
_____
_____

25 Questions and Phrases That Will Make Your Child Feel Valued by You

1. I love you.
2. I believe in you.
3. Be patient.
4. I trust you.
5. I respect you.
6. This is my expectation of you.
7. No.
8. Thank you.
9. I'm proud of you.
10. You are talented.
11. I admire you.
12. What do you think about...?
13. Let's hang out!
14. You are a leader.
15. Let's pray together.
16. I need your help with something.
17. How can I support you in achieving your dreams?
18. What brings you fulfillment?
19. How can I serve you?
20. Tell me about your most trusted friend.
21. What are your thoughts on romantic relationships?
22. What are your thoughts on illegal drugs?
23. What are your thoughts on charity?
24. Let's get something to eat.
25. Let's go shopping.

Bonus: I'm honored to be your father.
Bonus: God loves you.

About the Author

Jesse A. Cole, Jr. is a professional speaker, author, and leadership coach dedicated to empowering faith-driven influencers to lead with authenticity and boldness. As the founder of the Kingdom Confidence™ Movement, he equips professionals to lead unapologetically in life and business. With over 15 years of experience in education, sales, and nonprofit leadership, Jesse has worked with organizations like Ford Chaplains, Deloitte, Michigan State University, American Business Women Association, Kingdom Driven Entrepreneurs, and Americorps, helping leaders optimize their purpose and impact. The publisher of seven books, he has been featured in over 150 national and digital publications. His passion is to encourage and equip leaders by delivering spirit-led coaching that fosters confidence, authenticity, and an elevated mindset that produces transformation. When he's not speaking or facilitating trainings, Jesse enjoys watching documentaries and cherishing time with his wife and children.

More of Jesse Cole's Leadership Resources

Available on Amazon.com

BOOKING INFORMATION

Are you looking for an inspiring keynote speaker or transformational coach to empower your organization, school district, or leadership team? Let's connect!

Speaking & Workshops

✓ **Keynote Speeches** – Powerful and engaging talks that inspire confidence, leadership, and ambition.

✓ **Workshops & Training** – Interactive and practical sessions designed to develop leaders and equip teams.

✓ **Student Leadership Programs** – Customizable programs to help students cultivate leadership skills and community impact.

Coaching & Consulting

✓ **One-on-One Coaching** – Personalized coaching to develop leadership, confidence, and vision.

✓ **Group Coaching** – Small-group coaching sessions for young leaders, educators, and leadership teams.

✓ **School & District Partnerships** – Tailored programs for institutions investing in long-term student success.

Let's Work Together!

To inquire about booking, availability, and custom workshops, contact:

Jesse A. Cole, Jr.
info@CoachJesseCole.com
www.CoachJesseCole.com
(810) 354-5464

www.ingramcontent.com/pod-product-compliance
Lightning Source LLC
Chambersburg PA
CBHW051707090426
42736CB00013B/2587